Heavenly Realm Publishing

Houston, Texas

ISBN—13: 9781937911-77-5 (paperback)
ISBN—13: 978-1-937911-78-2 (ebook)

Library of Congress Control Number: 2014946538
The Power of the Holy Spirit: *For Those who Question, Need, and Want Understanding of the Power of the Holy Spirit/* Stephanie Franklin

This book is printed on acid free paper.

Printed in the United States of America

Religion: Christian Life- Inspirational—United States. 2. Religion: Christian Life- Personal Growth—United States. 3. Religion: Christianity-General—United States.

Published By: Heavenly Realm Publishing
P. O. Box 682532
Houston, TX 77268
www.heavenlyrealmpublishing.com
Toll Free 1-866-216-0696

Stephanie Franklin
Stephanie Franklin Ministries
info@stephaniefranklinministries.org
www.stephaniefranklin.org

The Power Of the Holy Spirit

For Those who Question, Need and
Want Understanding of the
Power of the Holy Spirit

Stephanie Franklin

THE POWER OF THE HOLY SPIRIT

For those who question, need, and want understanding of the power of the Holy Spirit.

THE POWER OF THE HOLY SPIRIT BRINGS:

> The Gifts:
> 1. *Knowing the Gifts*
> 2. *Operating in the Gifts*
> 3. *Why We as Christians & the Church Need Them*

*"But ye shall receive power, after the Holy Ghost
is come upon you: and ye shall be witnesses unto me
both in Jerusalem, and in all Judaea,
and in Samaria, and unto the uttermost part of the earth."*

Acts 1:8

"The Holy Spirit is given to those who ask for it."

Luke 11:13

*"Now the God of hope fill you with all joy and peace
in believing that ye may abound in hope, through the
power of the Holy Ghost (Spirit)."*

Romans 15:13

OTHER BOOKS BY STEPHANIE

The Power of the Holy Spirit

Introduction

God has been ministering to me about the Holy Spirit for quite some time now. He has ministered to me about many Christian Believers and non-Christian Believers who really do not understand the Who the Holy Spirit is. If you know Who the Holy Spirit is, you will know that He is not just One makeup of Heaven. The Holy Spirit is made up of the Godhead—three persons and they all are one together—God the Father, God the Son, and God the Holy Spirit. Each is eternally existence into one person. There is not One that is greater than the other. You believe in One, you believe in them all.

To understand the Holy Spirit, one must first understand Who the Father is. The Father is God Who created the entire universe, everything in it and its entire being. He is Jesus Christ who sits at the right side of the Father, which makes intercession for our daily groanings that we cannot comprehend (Hebrew 7:25-26). God is Jesus Christ who came in the flesh in His own image in order to lower Himself that man might believe and have a chance to eternal life. He is as Himself in Spirit and He lives within those who belong to Him (John 14:17-18, 26). He promised He will be with us always (John 14-16, emphasis on 14:15-26). All things are of God, who have reconciled all those who believe. Jesus Christ came on this earth to pave the way and to give us the ministry of reconciliation—we have a second chance to life and our sins to be forgiven through grace and mercy (2 Corinthians 5:18).

We must understand that we cannot get to the Father unless we first come through Jesus Christ, Who died for our sins, and three days later He rose again from death to eternal life; leaving us His Holy Spirit. Now we can as Christians who accept Jesus into our heart, mind, spirit, and soul can be confident that we no longer die to satan, but we obtain eternal life through Jesus Christ, Who paid the price for all of us who believe in Him. Romans 10:9 states, *"That if thou shalt confess with thy mouth the Lord Jesus, and shalt believe in thine heart that God raised him from the dead, thou shalt be saved."* After the Unbeliever verbally confesses this scripture and believe in his or her heart that God raise Jesus from the dead, you can be confident that you are saved and on your way to Heaven.

The *"Power of the Holy Spirit"* is not only providing knowledge on the Holy Spirit, but it is speaking on the **POWER** that the Holy Spirit has. The human flesh does not have the ability to be able to comprehend the **POWER** that the Holy Spirit brings. It takes the Spirit of God that lives on the inside of us to understand. This Spirit, which is the Spirit of God, can only be obtained by asking.

Introduction

In the book of Acts, chapter 2, verses 1-4, clarifies the comment I just made. The Scriptures explains that the apostles and others were gathered together on one accord, praying (asking) and believing together that God would fill them with His precious Holy Spirit. As they were praying together, the Bible says that suddenly there came a sound from Heaven as of a mighty rushing wind, which filled the house where they were all sitting, and they were all filled with the Holy Spirit. You must understand that He is yours as you ask for Him. Jesus Christ wants you to ask for Him. He wants to draw closer to you. There is a difference between just being saved (born again), and have accepted Jesus Christ as Lord and Savior in your life, than with having both, Salvation and the Baptism of the Holy Spirit. Salvation gets you into Heaven and allows you belong to Christ as a born again Believer. Whereas, the Holy Spirit allows you to abide in the presence of the Almighty God. He allows you be convicted to do right verses doing wrong. He gives you wisdom and insight into God's World, He brings comfort when you need Him, He directs your life and life's decisions, and most of all He allows you to know that Jesus Christ is with you always by His awesome presence. As you put them both together, there is an indescribable life changing combination. He is a linking, locking combination that cannot be broken by man, He can only be broken by you through disobedience and the lack of believing in God. There is no way around it, every Believer whether you just got saved, or whether you have been saved all your life, need the Holy Spirit.

The power of the Holy Spirit brings power. That power is not trusted in everybody. He is only trusted and will dwell in those who ask for Him, and are serious with faith to believe that He will rest within them all the days of their lives. That power is able to break and tear down everything that gets in His way. He is able to destroy every stronghold that may have you bound. He is able to bring truth to a lost and dying world. He is able to bring understanding to those who are lost and discouraged. He is able and ready to give insight and help to those who need it, and just to make it through each day. God is the Father, He is the Son, and He is the Holy Spirit. Experience the Holy Spirit through this teaching today.

CHAPTER ONE

Assurance of Knowing Who the Holy Spirit Is

The Promise of the Holy Spirit -John 14:15-31
God is our Comforter, which is the Holy Spirit. He is
the way, the truth, and the life (John 14:6, 14:1-13).

We have an assurance through God's Word who the Holy Spirit is. The Holy Spirit is several things. He is a Keeper. He is Peace. He is Hope when there is none. And, most of all, He is God the Father, God the Son, and God the Holy Spirit. He is One person, eternally existence into three persons.

He is the True Vine (John 15).

Jesus allows us to know in John 15:1 that He is the True Vine. He allows us to know that everything within us, He purges so that it will bring forth more fruit. This allows us to be clean from all that is not like Him. This can only be done if you abide in Him. He states in John 15:7 that, *"If you abide in me, and my words abide in you, you shall ask what you will and it shall be done unto you."* You cannot abide in God's presence, one on one with Him except you bear fruit. And, we all know that fruit is sweet. It is not soar. It is sweet and except you bear this type of fruit, you cannot abide in His presence, nor can you do anything. When you abide in the presence of the Holy Spirit with the Lord, you can ask whatever you will and it shall be done. If you need healing in your body, mind, Spirit, relationship(s), marriage, friendship(s), on your job, etc., the Word of God says it shall be done for you. I can recall a time when I was in prayer, abiding in the presence of the Holy Spirit, God spoke to me and said, *"I am removing the hurt from you."* I could not understand why He would say this because I did not feel hurt at the time of my communion with Him. But immediately He made me remember what I was hurt about and that I had to release it. I then recognized that it is impossible to abide with the Father when there is hurt, anger, malice, and hidden iniquity. You must first remove those things by repentance and then go before the Father as He cleanses you and speaks to you.

After you completely commit your life unto God, there is an excitement. There is a zeal and a hunger to get all you can from Him. You want to purchase every Christian book, CD, and/or DVD you can about the Bible. Your attitude is like "I don't want nobody else, all I want is Jesus." It is typical and it is normal. Many can agree that it is an awesome and life changing thing to give your life to God totally and to dwell in His presence. Christians who dwell in God's presence often weep as the result of experiencing His presence. Confirmation comes as the result of His presence. Love comes as the result of His presence. God is our everything. He understands us better than we understand ourselves. You never have to worry about not being able to trust Him because He's always there and He's always listening, and He's always trust worthy. Jesus is the True Vine, continue to commit your life to Him and abide in Him.

You may ask how do I abide in God's presence? Below are some steps in how to abide in God's presence:

1. You must first experience the Baptism of the Holy Spirit (Acts 2:1-4).

2. Get alone with God (in your room, prayer closet, or a closed area where you are totally alone with God) (Psalm 51:11).

3. Begin to thank Him and worship Him for Who He is (You may say it and you may also sing) (John 4:24).

4. Listen and wait for Him to speak first. (You may often hear God speak in an audible way, in a still small voice, or in a deep feeling and voice from within your soul) (John 10:27).

The Baptism of the Holy Spirit (John 1:26-33).
Now a days, much of the world does not care to know about the Holy Spirit, where He comes from, nor the reason why it is important to have Him. They operate on daily will of just getting by without any thought none what so ever.

There was a time in my life when I thought just like the world today. I could care less about the things of God and everything that came with it. However, one day after eating candy and passing notes in the back of a church my mom took my siblings and I to regularly, God touched me in such a convicted way that I began to cry and ran up to the altar and gave my life to the Lord. I was fourteen years old at the time. I received salvation that Sunday at that local church. They took me back in the back and read some literature to me and asked me did I believe in Jesus Christ and I said yes and I made my confession only with my mouth but not with my heart. I did believe in my heart that Jesus Christ did die on the cross and rose again to give me eternal life; and forgave me of all my sins. I received salvation but the need for the Baptism of the Holy Spirit was missing. It did not help that it was a traditional Baptist church and did not really teach much on the Baptism of Holy Spirit. So, it was foreign to me. I was still very young but understood salvation and the importance of needing it.

Years later, in my late teens, something inside of me lacked an empty void that could not be filled by man. I began to want more and could not figure out what it was. At the time, I'll call it, "something within me." I was unsettled and unsatisfied. I did not think about it too much because I was in my early years in college, starting a new life away from my family, and was a little nervous of the unknown of being at a big university away from them. As a result, the thought of dwelling on that feeling became void after things began to jump off and my new start got on the way.

As more years past, and after I settled in and got a routine, that same feeling came back to me, but this time worse. There was a yearning and a desire to draw closer to God. I can recall sometime back when a friend I had before leaving for college whose parents and family, at the time, were very religiously traditional in their belief, which was different than mine. They told me the only way I could make it to Heaven was if I spoke with other tongues. It made me very afraid but I trusted what they told me because I wanted so badly to make it to Heaven and thought, I'd better get what they got so I can make it. So, I practiced and practiced but was only babbling with my tongue and thought, if this is the way to Heaven, how many are up there? It was a challenge for me to maneuver my tongue the way they were as I visited their church and bible study from time to time. It did not help the fact that I did not read the Bible nor had little knowledge of the truth of the Bible, so I believed everything they told me. I practiced day and night until I became frustrated, troubled, and weary. They would ask me questions that I could not answer and to sing songs of worship that I did not understand but liked. They were really nice people but I just could not understand why in the world would God expect such of a great expectation if He wanted everybody in this great big ol' world to make it to Heaven? With that said, I became very confused to a point where I was afraid of going to church with her and her family. But then, that same thought and yearning that I felt years back that I could not fight off, was still pondering and pondering within me that I still was not sure of, kept me going to try to get what I felt that I needed. Well, it didn't work. I was still confused and still babbling at the mouth. I was sad that if I died that day, I was not going to make it to Heaven with the assurance of knowing that God would take in consideration that one thing was not done. Just when I was about to give up, one of the Christian brothers who was invited to their bible study one day, who was a boyfriend of my friend's friend, which was of another religion and faith than theirs, walked up to me and said something so profound that still sticks with me to this very day. The words he spoke were not deep, not religious words, but they were straight to the point. He said, *"Don't worry, when it is time, you will get it. Ask God and believe that you have it."* Those were his words in so many ways. Those words gave me the peace that I needed from that day forward to be confident, just believe, and be assured that God does not wish that anybody go to hell, and that He will make everything possible for the unbeliever to come to Christ. John 3:16 backs this statement up as it says,

> *"God so loved the world that He gave His only begotten*
> *Son, that whosoever believes in Him should not perish,*
> *but have everlasting life."*
> **John 3:16**

This Scripture is so profound in faith because it gives those who are struggling, and are confused as to whether or not they have to do unordinary things in order to see Heaven and to receive clarity and understanding. God says in His Word, all we have to do is make the confession with our mouth and **BELIEVE** in our hearts that Jesus was raised from the dead, and we shall be saved (Romans 10:9). If we just call on the Name of Jesus we shall be saved (Acts 2:21). Now this sounds like making it to Heaven to me. How bout' you? I will not bash my friend and her family for their faith at that time, but I shared the true story just to bring clarity if you are going through the same thing and are searching for the truth. All you have to do is believe, accept Jesus as your Lord and Savior, and by totally surrendering your will and giving your life to Him. Jesus in many ways encouraged and stressed this through His teachings within these books: Matthew, Mark, Luke, and John for the people to believe. When you believe, the Holy Spirit is not far away.

> *"Therefore I say unto you, What things soever ye desire,*
> *when ye pray, believe that ye receive them,*
> *and ye shall have them."*
> **Mark 11:24**

My life began to move forward and years past. I still desired and needed more knowledge on the Baptism of the Holy Spirit because I had not yet received Him.

The turnaround. God began to use people to invite me to church and to different church functions. All of which were speaking about receiving the Holy Spirit with the evidence of speaking in other tongues. The more I began to inquire, the more God began to bring me true knowledge through His Word. Sharing this brings me to say, that you cannot be assured of anything if you do not know what to be assured of. I could not be assured of knowing that I could have the Holy Spirit live within me by just asking for it. The Word of God speaks in Luke 11:13 that our *"...Heavenly Father gives the Holy Spirit to them that ask him."* I could not ask, and did not know to ask because I did not know that I could and what to ask. I was not knowledgeable of the Word and was not close to God in order to hear Him speak to me through His Holy Spirit. When you are unknowledgeable about anything, you will believe and fall for anything, especially if it sounds good. My friend's faith sounded good at the time because I did not have knowledge and did not know what the Word of God stated. I will encourage anybody that it is important to know what the Word of God (the Bible) says about any information you are confused about. If you are still not sure, it is important to not allow this powerful information to pass you by, you should go to your local church and talk to your pastor, youth pastor, knowledgeable leader, spiritual, or God sent mentor. If they are truly hearing from God, they will be able to help you to understand. It is God's Will that we understand the Bible and as the Word of God speaks in Hosea 4:6, that we do not perish for lack of knowledge.

I did receive the Baptism of the Holy Spirit in 1994, and have the evidence of speaking with other tongues (Heavenly language) (Acts 2:4). I now understand and enjoy God's presence and His precious Holy Spirit. I encourage you to experience Him too.

CHAPTER TWO

The Confidence on How to Receive and Value the Holy Spirit

Most Christians who have just made their Christian relationship with the Lord official often times lack confidence on how to receive and value the Holy Spirit. I certainly am not leaving out those who have been saved for over a period of time either. There are cases where the Christian Believer believes that it is not necessary to have the Holy Spirit and salvation is all you need. This is true to a certain extent. Salvation is needed in order to see the Lord and to be with Him in Heaven when your time expires here on earth. However, receiving the Holy Spirit helps you while on your Christian journey before your time expires.

Often times when a Christian Believer lack the Holy Spirit, you will see him or her quickly going back in sin or living sinful lives willfully with no conviction. The Holy Spirit brings conviction. He will convict you when you are wrong, when you are doing wrong, and when you are going in the wrong direction. I have found that most churches do not teach on the Holy Spirit but settle with salvation as the only key to a relationship with the Lord. Heaven has several keys and nuggets, and the baptism of the Holy Spirit is one of them. Churches who do not teach on this important subject have a fear of losing their congregation because they lack knowledge, do not prepare ministry leaders, and have fear of confusing the congregation's learning. We are all encouraged as Christian Believers, especially as pastors and Christian leaders to learn, lean, rely, and teach on the Baptism of the Holy Spirit. To be baptized in the Holy Spirit is to take off the old clothes and put on new clothes for the Lord. Please understand what I mean when I say old clothes. I am speaking of your old sinful way of life—your old sinful past and ungodly way of doing things and actions. It means to become a new creature in Christ and replace your old past and become a totally new person. You must understand that this is not a physical transformation; it is an inner Spiritual transformation. When you go down in the water and come out of the water, you are a totally new person in Christ. Please take note, it is not the water that changes you, it is God's Spirit that changes you, and you feel completely brand new. If you have been born again, please share your testimony. It will change someone's life. If you have not, please do not be discouraged, ask God for the Holy Spirit, give yourself to constant prayer on receiving it, and wait because it will not be long before God fills you with it. You can also go and speak to your local church (pastor, leader, youth or young adult leader, Spiritual mentor or counselor).

The Holy Spirit is our teacher and our Comforter. In John chapter 14, verses 15-31, Jesus was speaking to the disciples about the promise of the Holy Spirit as a Comforter. Jesus was stating that He will give them a Comforter and that He would be with them always in Spirit, and He will dwell among them and abide within them. That same Spirit that Jesus left for them is the same Spirit He has left for us. We are considered God's disciples too. When you confessed and accepted Jesus as Lord and Savior of your life, you became His disciple—you are to go out in the world (your home, school, job, community, lost family and friends, etc.) and share your faith of Jesus Christ and draw other unbelievers to Christ.

Jesus says in verse 18 of that same chapter in John that He will never leave us comfortless. If Jesus had left us without leaving us His Holy Spirit, we would not have a guide or a teacher. We would not feel and know that He is with us. We would try to rely on books, literature, and word of mouth, but it would not be the same as being a personal experience for yourself. Jesus knew this and this is why He said that He would never leave us comfortless. Jesus knew that we would need to feel Him when we go through hard times (death in the family or friends, problems in relationships) and would need someone to comfort us like no other human could. We would need our Father in Heaven to be with us and to give us peace and to comfort our hearts to know that He is with us as He promised. God is the same with you and you can be confident at knowing that He is with you no matter what. It does not matter if no one is with you and you feel all alone, and feel as if no one understands your situation, or the torment and confusion you feel inside, you can be confident today that the Holy Spirit is within you and He will never leave you nor will He ever forsake you (Hebrews 13:5). This is an assurance to know that you do not have to fight your battles alone because He is there.

After you have received the Baptism of the Holy Spirit, you can value Who He is and Where He comes from. Before you were born again, you could not value the Holy Spirit because you were blind and could not see the truth. However, now that you have obtained knowledge, you can value Him and embrace Him and be confident to know that He is with you and lives deep down on the inside of you.

How Do I Value the Holy Spirit? (John 14)
1. You must first learn and know Who the Holy Spirit is and where He lives.
2. You must then have received the Holy Spirit.
3. You can be confident of Who the Holy Spirit is and where He lives.
4. You must be confident and value the Holy Spirit.

You do not have to be afraid of the Holy Spirit (John 14:27). I guarantee you that He will not hurt or harm you. In fact, when you receive Him, you will be wanting more and more of Him. In the Word of God it states in John 14:26, that the Comforter, which is the Holy Ghost, whom the Father sends in Jesus' Name, will teach you all things and bring all things to your remembrance. God will give you all you need and you do not have to be troubled or afraid because you do not have Him or depressed because you do not know how to get Him. You do not have to be jealous of others who have Him and you do not at this moment. God sees where you are and He is coming to give you what you have asked of Him, but you have to be patient in this short season while God is moving for you. I remember when I had just gotten saved, and was excited about sharing my testimony and anxious about being used by God, there were others around me who had the Holy Spirit and I did not. I so wanted what they had and did not know how to get Him. I was not satisfied nor was I comfortable about not having Him. I wanted and desired Him. You notice I said "wanted and desired?" You have to want Him and desire to have Him on the inside of you. The Holy Spirit will not come if you do not want Him, and do not have a desire to have Him on the inside of you. God knows when you are truthful, verses just doing and saying something. He knows when you are telling the truth. So make sure that you are truthful with yourself and God and really want to receive from Him. Amen? Praise God. God desires that you have Him on the inside of you. He desires to be close to you in any way He can. He desires to commune with you on a daily basis. You can be confident in knowing this. And, as you are confident in knowing this, you can value what you know by simply just allowing God to have His way.

THE TABERNACLE

The Tabernacle is a part of the Holy Spirit. It is where God dwelt with His people Israel. God says in Exodus 25:8, *"Have them make me a sanctuary, so that I may dwell among them."* So here, the tabernacle was a means in which God's sacrificial, holy presence in Spirit could dwell among His sinful people. It was a way to maintain fellowship with them. As a symbol of His presence, it would be that He came in person of his Son to visibly dwell (His presence) with his people in John 1:14. You must understand the importance of regarding the tabernacle as Holy ground. In Exodus 3:5, God quicken Moses and told him to remove his shoes because he was standing on Holy ground. Also, you cannot go into the presence any kind of way. Many Christians in the tabernacle (the church) have become way too comfortable. Although God is not into what we wear or how we look, He looks at the heart, the Holy Spirit serves His part to convict us when we are dressing in a manner that will make other Christian brothers and sisters; and even non-Christians in the sanctuary uncomfortable. This can invite other spirits that are not of God in, and cause others to struggle rather than have their minds on Christ and His presence.

Technology (cell phones, iphones, tablets, etc.) have increased and have broadened the knowledge to a point where the Bible can be viewed through an application on these various devices.

There are some Christians who carry them into the sanctuary and use them as the pastor or leader speaks, teaches, and/or preaches. These items can cause a distraction. We as Christian Believers have to be careful because the enemy is tricky and sneaky, and he will use people as well as things to distract the Will of God and the presence of the Holy Spirit from dwelling and from operating effectively. Satan does not want the Will of God to go forth in the tabernacle, nor does he want God's Holy Spirit to shower down on God's people during that most precious, sacred, and holy time.

When the anointing and the presence of God is active among the Saints, this is when God is there and is in full operation to speak, teach, heal, deliver, direct, love, and prophesy. You must be careful not to allow devises and fashion to distract what could be the most powerful life changing moment of your life and others. I am in no means bashing churches who do use devises as a part of their worship and teaching among the congregation, I am simply stating that you must be careful not to allow these devises to distract the Will and purpose of God at that moment.

The altar is the most sacred and most Holiest place of the sanctuary. It is where God likes to do the most work before, during, and after service. I am in no way saying that God cannot touch or save a person in the church bathroom or anywhere else before, during, or after church service. I am saying that the altar is chosen to be the most Holiest—a place for salvation, healing, deliverance, restoration, reconciliation, and cleansing. In Exodus 28:43, the altar was considered the place of holiness. You had to be clean before entering in the tabernacle and the altar. If the priest were unclean and tried to enter in the tabernacle that way, they would die and have to be pulled out by a rope. To this day, it is important when prayer is going forth at the altar, that you watch your conversations, do not have fighting matches with each other, do not hold loud conversations around the altar, nor do you walk or step over those who have been prayed for and are slain in the spirit as they lay on the floor. To be slain in the Spirit is a spiritual experience where a person will fall to the floor because of a powerful, personal encounter between that person and the power of God. Often times it is associated with the laying on of hands. You may also hear falling out in the Spirit, falling out under the anointing, and laying on of hands. Each of these terms are the same and are accepted the same. It is important to regard and respect the altar as Holy ground and know that God lives there.

For more research and reading on the altar and it being considered Holy, you may read Leviticus 16:20-33.

CHAPTER THREE

Understanding the Holy Spirit

J esus is the perfect One for understanding the Holy Spirit. He is the true reason for the Holy Spirit. The Holy Spirit is "He". He is represented in three persons—God the Father, God the Son, and God the Holy Spirit.

To obtain knowledge, and understand the Holy Spirit is to:

1. Know the meaning of the Word.

2. Know the Spirit in relation to the Godhead.

3. Know the Spirit of God in Man.

4. Know the Heavenly Language.

5. Know the Outpouring of the Spirit.

Know the Meaning of the Word

As I have stated before, it is important to know the meaning of the Word, "Holy Spirit". The Holy Spirit is the Trinity—it is manifested as God the Father, God the Son, and God the Holy Spirit. Each of these are represented as God Himself. It is also associated with the Baptism of the Holy Spirit or Holy Ghost, generally associated with the Spiritual baptism of the washing of the Holy Spirit.

The phrase "Baptism of the Holy Spirit" is found in the New Testament:

John came and baptized in water but made it known that it was Jesus, the Lamb of God, Who baptize with the Holy Spirit (Holy Ghost). You may read below for further reference.

(26) "John answered them, saying, I baptize with water: but there standeth one among you, whom ye know not;

(27) He it is, who coming after me is preferred before me, whose shoe's latchet I am not worthy to unloose.

(28) These things were done in Bethabara beyond Jordan, where John was baptizing.

*(29) The next day John seeth Jesus coming unto
him, and saith, Behold the Lamb of God, which
taketh away the sin of the world.
(30) This is he of whom I said, After me cometh a
man which is preferred before me:
for he was before me.*

*(31) And I knew him not: but that he should be
made manifest to Israel, therefore am I come
baptizing with water.*

*(32) And John bare record, saying, I saw the Spirit
descending from heaven like a dove,
and it abode upon him.*

*(33) And I knew him not: but he that sent me to
baptize with water, the same unto me, Upon whom
thou shalt the Spirit descending, and remaining on
him, the same is he which baptizeth
with the Holy Ghost."*

John 1:26-33

Know the Spirit in Relation to the Godhead:

The Spirit in relation to the Godhead is God represented as One—God the Father, God the Son, and God the Holy Spirit. The Godhead represents the Divine Trinity—Father, Son, and Holy Spirit. God is all of these in One person.

For additional Biblical reference where "Godhead" is found, read Romans 1:20.

Know the Spirit of God in Man:

The Spirit of God in man is God placing His Spirit within man. In John 20:19-22 Jesus appears to the disciples and speaks to them. He makes reference to the Holy Spirit as He appears to them after He died on the cross and was buried in a tomb (verse 19). He comforts them by saying, *"peace be unto you"* and then He leaves them His Holy Spirit by breathing on them and says, *"receive the Holy Spirit"* (verse 22). This is evidence that God's Spirit is within man. As I refer to "man", I am referring to man and woman, boy and girl, child and baby—everyone. After you accept God as Lord and Savior and come into a personal relationship with Him, you have by faith become His child (one of His own). When you receive the Baptism of the Holy Spirit, you show evidence of His Spirit living inside of you. You are then considered as a man of God, a woman of God, or a child of God acting, speaking, and living in the image of God. You are never to consider yourself as God, but as a person who walks, talks, acts, and lives after the things of God.

Know the Heavenly Language:

To know the Heavenly language is to obtain the Holy Spirit with the evidence of speaking with other tongues. Tongues are considered as your Heavenly language—language between you and God. The Apostles and others in Acts 2:1-4, received the Holy Spirit with evidence of speaking with other tongues. This was evidence of God's Spirit resting on each of them as He gave them what they were all asking for, as they were all on one accord. He is yours as you ask for Him (Luke 11:13).

Know the Outpouring of the Spirit:

The Apostles and others received the outpouring of the Holy Spirit. The Word of God states in Acts 2:3-4, that as they were all on one accord, there came a sound from Heaven as of a mighty rushing wind and sat on each of them, as they were all filled with the Holy Ghost (Spirit), and began to speak in other tongues as the Spirit gave them utterance. We can say that this was a powerful move of God in that place. God poured His Spirit on them as He rested on each of them. The overwhelming presence of His power made them speak with other tongues. Have you ever experienced this in your life? I can recall when I first received the Holy Spirit with the evidence of speaking with other tongues, I could not stop weeping in God's presence. It was not a sad or angry cry, it was an awesome refreshing presence that was pleasing to my soul. He washed away all of my fears, disappointments, and had my mind completely caught up in Him. Nothing mattered. Nobody mattered. This is the outpouring of

His Spirit. When you experience His over and above and beyond, undying and unfailing presence, you will never be the same.

CHAPTER FOUR

The Ability to Maintain Self Control, Love,
Patience, Peace, and Humility (love) Once
the Holy Spirit is Received

Many times after the Christian Believer receives salvation along with the Holy Spirit, the attacks from satan begins. Satan never wants you to win. He does not want you to be close to God nor does he want you to belong to Him. This is why it is so important to get into a Bible based church ministry that will teach you the Bible, how to read your Bible on a daily basis, and center yourself around other strong Christian Believers. This will help you to get stronger, maintain your strength, gain knowledge on how to fight the enemy, and maintain your self-control, love, patience, peace, and humility in trying times.

It is biblically a known fact that the Holy Spirit is your Peace and Comforter. He promises to give you what you should say at that very moment when conflict rises up in your life. No one can avoid conflict, it is everywhere. However, I can tell you how to deal with it. The best way to deal with conflict is by allowing the Holy Spirit to control your tongue and give you what to say at that very moment (Luke 12:12). Allow the Holy Spirit to be in control within you not to burst into a burning rage or anger like other person(s) who will try to push you to your limit. Allow the Holy Spirit to give you wisdom and not allow those person(s) to get to you and make you sin with your mouth and actions (Ecclesiastes 5:6). This can be a terrible thing especially for the Christian believer who is supposed to be a Godly example (at home, in the work place, on vacation, at school—everywhere).

Reading your Bible on a daily basis will help you to maintain self-control, love, patience, peace, and humility (love) once the Holy Spirit is received.

The fruit of the Spirit should be your guide to help maintain self-control, love, patience, peace, and humility in your most humiliating moments. The fruit of the Spirit can be found in the book of Galatians, chapter 5, verses 22-23. It is considered love, joy, peace, longsuffering, gentleness, goodness, faith, meekness, and temperance. All of which must operate on a daily basis in order that conflict and opposition do not come your way. It is a hurtful thing to have just received the Baptism of the Holy Spirit and allow satan to come in and rob your celebration, and make you sin and lose respect of those who are watching you and possibly contemplating salvation for themselves. It is vital to rest in God's presence as much as possible so that you do not fall vulnerable or prey to the flesh and devilish things that will make you forget that you ever had the Holy Spirit in the first place. While no one is perfect, it is important to strive for perfection as much as possible.

CHAPTER FIVE

The Gift to Know Your Calling/Purpose Through the Holy Spirit

I t is imperative to know your gift and calling, considering it is God who gave it to you to use for His purpose and glory. Gifts and callings come without repentance, which means that we all have them (Romans 11:29). They were given to each of us before we were in our mother's womb. God strategically placed the gift or gifts inside of you to use for His purpose. You have a special work and assignment to do while here on this earth before your expiration (death—to leave the earthly body) date comes. The Holy Spirit comes as a guide and a Helper to help you discern right from wrong, get what you need, where you need to go, and what you need to do while on your journey here.

When you know what your gift or gifts are, be confident at knowing that it is God Who is using you and it is God Who has to be glorified at all times. God has given different Spiritual gifts for the edification of the church and the Saints of God. Each gift is to be used accordingly and for the purpose through the Holy Spirit.

Below are three steps on knowing, operating, and why you need them:

The Gifts:

1. Knowing the Gifts
2. Operating in the Gifts
3. Why We as Christians & the Church Need Them

1. **Knowing the Gifts:**
   The Spiritual gifts are (1 Corinthians 12:27-31):

   1. Gift to teach (The Word of knowledge)
   2. Gift of miracles
   3. Gift of healing
   4. Gift of helps
   5. Gift of governments (administration)
   6. Gift of diversities of tongues
   7. Gift of prophesy
   8. Gift of discernment
   9. Gift of faith
   10. Gift of love

2. Operating in the Gifts:

You must be careful to operate in the Spiritual gifts in a humble, wise, and God fearing way. All gifts from God does not belong to us. They are merely given to us <u>ONLY</u> for God's purpose. In all cases, they are used for the purpose of drawing the unbeliever to Christ. They are not to be played with or taken lightly. They are not to be used in an unethical or ungodly way. None of us has the right to operate within the gifts as we choose too. We must be obedient to the Holy Spirit as He leads before operating in any gift. There have been times when Christian Believers have abused this area to a degree that have made people afraid and leery of receiving from them. This should not be so. Before you operate in the gift(s), you should have already sought the leading of the Holy Spirit, gotten Word from God on how, where, when, who, and what to do. God will never lead you astray.

While God is not the author of confusion, it is imperative to use each gift as the Holy Spirit leads. There may not be a need for all of the gifts to be in operation at the same time. Therefore, the Holy Spirit will lead as the Spirit gives utterance.

3. **Why We as Christians & the Church Need Them (1 Corinthians 12, 14:12, entire chapter 12 and 14):**

Spiritual Gifts are given to the Christian and to the church for the edification and use of the Lord. In order to win souls for Christ, gifts are needed. Gifts are used for the Christian and the church who needs them for healing, deliverance, guidance, and so forth. While there is always room for improvement, Spiritual gifts are needed for this reason, which is to improve those areas of weakness so that satan cannot come in and operate against the Will of God. These Spiritual gifts also help the Christian Believer to maintain his or her salvation and positive walk with God.

Each of these are gifts through God's precious Holy Spirit for His edification, glory and use.

CHAPTER SIX

Rest in the Holy Spirit

*Let us therefore fear, lest, a promise being left us
of entering into his rest, any of you should
seem to come short of it.*

Hebrews 4:1

Resting in the Holy Spirit is not the same as resting in your bed at night. It is merely resting from worrying or being weary about the things of life. It is resting at the feet of Jesus. It is resting in God's presence until He decides to move in your situation. It is resting and totally trusting in His Word and promise.

I can recall a time when I was going through a tough time in my life and needed a Word from God and He spoke clearly to me and said, "rest". At that moment, it did not dawn on me what He was speaking about. I thought He was speaking of resting in my body by going to take a nap or to lie down for a while. But, God was speaking of resting from all of my troubles and totally leaning, relying, and trusting Him. This is why the scripture in Proverbs 3:5-6 is so popular, whereas, it states for us *"to lean not to our own understanding, but in all of our ways acknowledge Him and He will direct our path."* This was proof of rest for me. So, I encourage you to rest in the Lord. Let Him do His work and work out your situation that you are going through. Do not get in His way and try to handle the situation on your own. You cannot win going against God's Will and Plan. You will always fail and have to go back and do it again. So, do your best to do it right the first time by resting—getting back out of the way and allow God to be God.

Biblical Scriptures on Rest:

2 Thessalonians 1:7, When you are troubled about big or small problems, God encourages you to rest in Him.

Psalm 46:1, 5, 10, God is your present help in time of trouble. All you have to do is rest in His presence as He works it out for you. Jehoshaphat and all of Judah rested in God's presence, they were prophetically told to worship God while He make their enemies war against themselves by bringing ambushments against them (2 Chronicles 20:22) (2 Chronicles 20:1-30).

Matthew 11:28-30, God encourages the Christian Believer to come to Him, all those who labour and are heavy laden, who are down and feel defeated, to come to Him and find rest. He is also encouraging the Christian Believer to take His yoke upon them, and learn of Him, because He is meek and lowly in heart and you should find rest for your weary soul. His yoke is easy and it is light. There are no heavy burdens that He cannot solve. There are no afflictions that He cannot heal. There are no situations that He cannot get you out of. There are no enemies that He cannot protect you from. God's yoke (oppressions, burdens, load, and stress) is easy and it is light. God realizes that you will get overloaded and feel as though you want to quit, but He encourages you to come into His rest. God realizes that the road may seem long and getting to the end is unbearable, but I say hold on and keep pressing on as you <u>rest</u> in Him while He goes before you and make your way easier and lighter. He promises that He will take care of you. He will.

Mark 10:27 For with men, it is impossible, but with God all things are possible. There is nothing too hard for God. All you have to do is <u>rest</u> in Him while He do the impossible for you and your situation.

CHAPTER SEVEN

Experience the Power of the Holy Spirit

The power of the Holy Spirit is One (Father, Son, Holy Spirit) that cannot be described. He is an awesome presence and feeling that no one on this earth can duplicate. Once the Holy Spirit is experienced, you will never be the same. He is special in His own right.

The Holy Spirit serves as point of contact between the Christian Believer and God. It is easy to think of the Holy Spirit as being this supernatural being who has transcended into Heaven without any chance of residing here on earth. However, this is not true, He is very much so present within us (those who ask for Him). He has an important residence within our hearts, minds, Spirits, and souls. He is our constant communication to the Father.

Converted

When we think in terms of a person being converted we think of someone who has done something so detrimental and damaging that it would seem impossible for them to convert to something good from bad. With Christ, all things are possible. The Holy Spirit has the power to do anything but fail (Deuteronomy 31:8, Jeremiah 32:17, Luke 1:37). He has the power to change anybody. This is why we have often seen on television those who have shared their testimony of how they were once unbelievers, murderers, rapist, and many more that is too many to name. The Bible gives great reference on one that I want to highlight. You may be familiar with him as well. Let's talk about Paul, once known as Saul. The book of Acts, specifically in chapter 9:1-31, is so significant in speaking of this man who once hated Christians and sought to have them killed, but later after he was converted, was one of the most powerful witnesses for the Lord. It is powerful how God converted him as fast as He did. This is a prime example of how God, through the ministry of the Holy Spirit can take an unbeliever and deal with him or her one second, and the next make them a changed person. Ever experienced this? Or, do you know anybody who experienced this before? God did this very thing to Saul as He spoke to him, as Saul (Paul) trembled with fear and astonishment, and gave him specific instructions.

Not stopping there, but God went beyond the conversion and made Saul a Believer by making him blind and then healing him, letting Ananias know Saul (Paul) was the chosen one. Paul was not only converted, as we see in chapter 9:1-31, but we see he was also filled with the Holy Spirit (Acts 13:9). I encourage you to do further study on this chapter (Acts 9:1-31). God is no respect of persons, He can save and can fill anybody with His precious Holy Spirit, no matter what their past was.

Filled By Faith and Not By Emotions

The power of the Holy Spirit is much needed in times of affliction, weakness, and pain. When the Christian Believer goes through these types of situations, it brings on emotions that are generally not assigned by the Holy Spirit. There is much tension, doubt, and worry of how God will work things out, how He will get them out of their dilemmas, how He will help make things alright. These constitute emotions that are not written in the Word of God (tension, doubt, worry). The Holy Spirit will always minister peace to those who seek Him for it. The scripture in Romans 15:13 states, *"Now the God of hope fill with all joy and peace in believing, that ye may abound in hope, through the power of the Holy Ghost (Spirit)."* This scripture proves that God is hope and it is His desire to fill the Christian Believer with joy and peace along with faith in believing and abounding in hope through the Holy Spirit. We need the Holy Spirit. Without Him we will crash. This is why this scripture encourages the Believer to abound in God's hope and be filled with joy and peace through the power of the Holy Spirit, so that when affliction, weakness, and pain come, the Believer will count them all joy, be strong, and walk in the hope of peace.

It is not God's Will that the Christian Believer worry and carry all sorts of emotions that bring on other spirits that come to bound the Believer to doubt or even to unbelief. It is easy when things are going great with no pressure that we become complacent, and do not rely on the leading of the Holy Spirit for constant direction, advice, and peace. We try to handle things on our own, thinking that we can make it without the Holy Spirit, which is impossible. We will fail each time. It is encouraged that you hold on to God's joy and perfect peace through faith as you go through your daily walk each day.

The Holy Spirit is the Supernatural

To operate in the Supernatural is to operate and trust in the Heavenly unseen and the unknown. In Acts, chapter 2:1-4, we find that something supernatural happened when they (the Apostles and others) were all on one accord and the Holy Ghost (Spirit) sat on them all like tongues of fire. This was the supernatural. They believed in something that would seem unsure to come. However, because they all believed, had faith, and were all on one accord, He came and not only did He sit on each of them, but He filled each of them with the precious Holy Ghost (Spirit).

The supernatural can happen in good times and in bad times in our lives. There is no certain time or day, or certain situation. Most times it comes when God tests the Believer to believe and to trust Him to bring their need to past in a way that it would only take God to do it as He gets full glory. One great example is Hezekiah in 2 Kings 20:1-11, as he was sick unto death. God sent the prophet Isaiah to tell Hezekiah to get his house in order and to tell his family that he was going to die. Immediately when Hezekiah heard the news, he set himself to seek God. As he inquired of the Lord, worshipped Him, reminded God of how he'd been faithful to Him in the past, and petitioned that He spare his life, God quickly spoke to Hezekiah through the prophet Isaiah and told him that He would give Hezekiah additional years of life. This was the supernatural. God changed His mind **IMMEDIATELY** and gave Hezekiah just what he was asking for. So, in this situation, what seemed bad was turned into something good as we see that God is sovereign to hear our petitions and make changes to our benefit, **IMMEDIATELY**. This shows that God can change His mind

IMMEDIATELY in your life. It should be in your faith to believe, and not accept anything, but to take God at His every Word and His covenant (promise) (Psalm 20:5).

Experiencing the Power of the Holy Spirit:
Listening and Yielding Yourself

Most times the Holy Spirit does not come because the Believer does not listen or does not yield him or herself to receive it. In order to experience the power of the Holy Spirit, the Christian Believer must have a yearning desire to have it. There must be an obedient yearning to yield to His Spirit. As you yield your life through obedience, seek His face, and let Him come in, you will experience the power of the Holy Spirit.

The Holy Spirit, the Living Waters

The Holy Spirit, the living waters refers to the Holy Spirit as the living water, that if you drink it (Him), you will never thirst again. As we look in John, chapter 4, verses 6-15, Jesus was tired from his journey to Samaria and decided to sit at a well as the disciples went to town to buy meat. A woman of Samaria came to draw water from the well as Jesus asked for a drink of water. The woman questioned, as she was shocked that Jesus would ask such a thing because He was a Jew, and Jews did not like the Samaritans. Jesus quickly answered her, *"If thou knew the gift of*

God, and who it is that saith to thee, Give me to drink; thou wouldest have asked of him, and he would have given thee living water" (John 4:10). A significant point here is that Jesus does not mention that He is the living water, but that He would give living water to her, and when she receive it, she would never thirst again. Further, in the text, it gives a more in depth look on this powerful subject in John 7:37-39. In this passage of scripture, Jesus is in the temple and cries out, *"if any man thirst, let him come unto me, and drink. (38) He that believeth on me, as the scripture hath said, out of his belly shall flow rivers of living water."* In this situation as the scripture tells us in verse 39, that Jesus *"spoke of the Spirit (the Holy Spirit), which they that believe on him should receive: for the Holy Ghost (Spirit) was not yet come; because Jesus was not yet glorified."*

As the scriptures above lets us know, the living waters clearly are speaking of the Holy Spirit. Many would say that Jesus is the living water, but here it is the Holy Spirit is the living water, as He rest on the inside of the Christian Believer. It is through your faith and belief as a Christian Believer that the ministry of the Holy Spirit brings you New Life and redeems those who are lost from the enemy as He brings life and light to them.

The Holy Spirit is like a well that never runs dry. He is the Bread of Life and He is everlasting to everlasting, even until the end of the earth. Jesus is almighty, and He sits high and looks low. None can compare to Him and His greatness. He is El Shaddai, God Almighty. He is Elohim, He is God. You two, can experience the Holy Spirit Who is the living water, just ask for Him, and after you receive Him, you will never run out. You will never thirst again.

Conclusion

The Power of the Holy Spirit comes to bring clarity and understanding to those who may not understand or fully understand What, and Who the Holy Spirit is. Some believe that it is only important to confess the Lord Jesus into their life and that is all to be saved. And, yes that may be true. However, that is not all to salvation. The Holy Spirit comes to live inside of you as you go through this life and on your Christian journey. The Baptism of the Holy Spirit washes you clean from your old past, and makes you spiritually brand new.

If you are one that have never heard of the Holy Spirit, hopefully and prayerfully you now have clear insight and understanding on Who He is, why He came, and His purpose after reading this book, *The Power of the Holy Spirit*. I encourage you to do further study on the Holy Spirit (Holy Ghost) in Acts 19:1-6.

You now have the opportunity to receive salvation as you ***confess with your mouth and truly believe in your heart that God raised Jesus from the dead,*** the Bible says that you shall be saved. Right now, I believe that if you verbally confess those bold words and truly mean them in your heart, **you are now saved**. Now my prayer is that the power and the Baptism of the Holy Spirit will rest, rule, and abide within you and that you will never be the same. Amen.

STEPHANIE FRANKLIN, M. Th.

Obtains a Master of Arts degree in Theological Studies and has a vision to reach the world with her mentoring, teaching, life coaching, and preaching ministry. She has a heart to reach the youth and young adults along with the entire family, bringing them all together as a unified fold. One of her greatest desires is to be used by God in whatever capacity He chooses.